W9-AFJ-786

SELF-MADE STATIONERY

SELF-MADE STATIONERY

KAZUMI UDAGAWA

HANDMADE GOODS DESIGNED BY ME

©2008 by Kazumi Udagawa

All rights reserved. No part of this book may be reproduced in any form without written permission of the copyright owners. All images in this book have been reproduced with the knowledge and prior content of the artists concerned and no responsibility is accepted by producer, publisher, or printer for any infringement of copyright or otherwise, arising from the contents of this publication. Every effort has been made to ensure that credits accurately comply with information supplied.

First published in 2008 in Japan by
Ikeda Shoten Publishing Co., Ltd.
43 Benten-cho, Shinjuku-ku, Tokyo 162-0851, Japan
www.ikedashoten.co.jp
under the title of Tedukuri Bunbougu

First published in 2009 in the United States of America by
Quarry Books, a member of
Quayside Publishing Group
100 Cummings Center
Suite 406-L
Beverly, Massachusetts 01915-6101
USA
Phone: 987-282-9590
Fax: 978-283-2742
www.rockpub.com

English translation rights arranged with
Ikeda Shoten Publishing Co., LTD.
through Rico Komanoya, ricorico, Tokyo, Japan.

Translation: Naoko Hirase
Copy-editing: Alma R. H. Reyes
Art direction: Katsuya Moriizumi, Takuji Segawa (Killigraph)
Book Design : Katsuya Moriizumi
Editing: Mick Nomura, Takuji Segawa (Killigraph), Kaoru Tanabe
Photographs: Etsuko Miyasaka
Illustrations and Styling: Kazumi Udagawa
Photo collaboration: transista (www.transista.jp/)
Production: Aki Ueda (ricorico)
Chief editor and producer: Rico Komanoya (ricorico)

ISBN-13: 978-1-59253-544-6
ISBN-10: 1-59253-544-5

10 9 8 7 6 5 4 3 2 1

Printed in China by Everbest Printing Co., Ltd.

CONTENTS

* = Easy-to-make Stationery Items

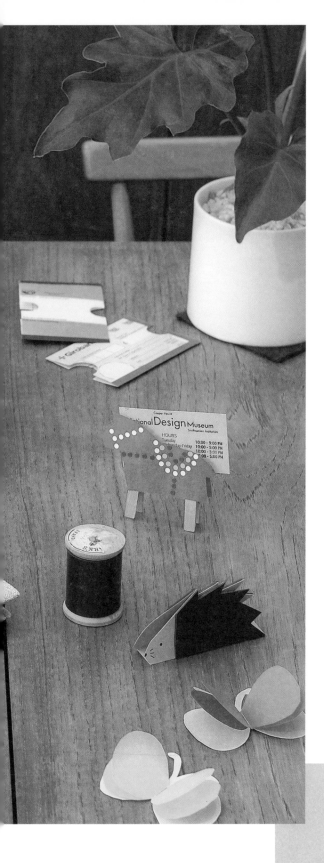

INTRODUCTION:
What is Self-made Stationery?

Sometimes, when you write down your daily schedule in your diary, don't you wish that you had more space to write on? When I think of this, I make a small notebook and paste it to my diary, creating a book within a book. It has become my habit, since I was in college, to customize my diaries to fit my needs. This motivated me to start creating handmade stationery and book crafts.

Whenever I see stationery material or other paper products at stores, I would think that I could make them by myself rather than buy them. To be able to make something by yourself is to create original goods of your desired size and style that cannot be found anywhere else in the world. When you need some stationery, take a look at the samples in this book before you go to the stationery shop.

The measurements of the stationery items introduced in this book are not fixed, but serve as guide. You may change the sizes freely to meet your needs.

Once you start making your own stationery or book crafts, you will find them indispensable, and you will want to use them for as long as you can. So, why not start making your own favorite stationery now!

Easy-to-make Stationery Items

Creating simple stationery items in five minutes
I designed some easy-to-make stationery items for those who are too busy to do paper craft. You can make any of these items from thirty seconds to five minutes using everyday materials found in your home. Even if you are not good at making things, you can try making one of the sample items presented in this section.

USEFUL TOOLS

Scissors
Use scissors to cut any material. Coated scissors are recommended, so that when you need to use glue, it does not stick.

Craft Knife
Use a craft knife to cut paper in a straight line. To cut cardboard, cut three to four times, as if you are tracing the line.

Rotary Cutter
A rotary cutter is convenient for cutting fabric more sharply than scissors. You can also use a zigzag-edge rotary cutter.

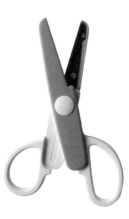

Pinking Shears
Use pinking shears to cut paper in a zigzag pattern. Don't use fabric pinking shears because the blades will be ruined.

Glue and Glue Tape Dispenser
A glue stick is easy to handle; also a glue tape dispenser can be convenient.

Pattern Wheel
A pattern wheel can be used to make pierced patterns.

Pricker

This is a common Japanese kimono dressmaking tool that is good for making holes, plotting measurements, and marking tiny dots on paper.

Double-sided Adhesive Tape

Double-sided adhesive tape is the most frequently used tool for stationery making, and is easier to use than glue. It easily functions as a seal. Tapes of 2 in (50 mm) and 0.75 in (20 mm) wide are useful.

Bookbinding Tape

Bookbinding tape can be used to reinforce the spine of a notebook or the corners of a box. A colored bookbinding tape can accentuate the total design of your product, especially if you match the colors of the body and the tape.

Eyelets

Eyelets are stylish and can be good design accessories. You also need an eyelet puncher.

Rubber Stamps

It is fun to use rubber stamps of various shapes and designs, such as alphabets, numbers, a crown motif, bird cage, and more.

Puncher

Use a puncher to make holes.

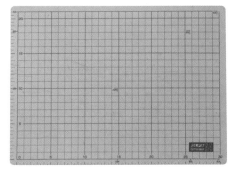

Cutting Mat

A cutting mat is indispensable for cutting paper. A mat of A4 size or 8 in x 11 in (210 mm x 297 mm) is useful.

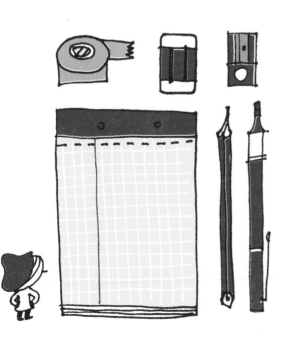

USEFUL MATERIALS

Envelopes
I prefer bunched envelopes to a letter set. I usually buy 20 to 50 pieces each of different sizes, paper types, and purposes.

Paper
Keep a stock of various types of paper, like colored Kent paper, origami paper, wrapping paper, craft paper, maps of foreign countries, and others.

Buttons
Buttons and paper are a good combination. You can use buttons tied with strings. I personally enjoy shopping for antique buttons.

Magnet Sheet
Use a plain, adhesive-type magnet sheet that can easily be cut. You can make your original magnet stickers by affixing postage stamps on them.

Cardboard
I often buy yellowish cardboard paper and keep the thick cardboard base that comes with the package. It is preferable to use a thick and sturdy type of cardboard paper.

Paper Fasteners
Paper fasteners are useful for fastening and folding pieces of paper. You can use a paper fastener to attach the rubber band used for making Card-Size Folders, as shown on page 40-41.

Patterned Fabric
Use a wide variety of fabrics, such as those with lovely patterns, like cloth food bags, Japanese tenugui (smooth face towel), or a piece of tablecloth. I've also used curtains that I bought at a flea market abroad.

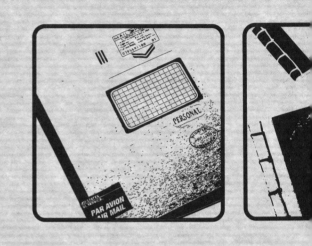

CHAPTER 1
NOTEBOOKS AND MEMO ACCESSORIES

RUBBER BAND NOTEBOOK

It's simple to make a casual-style notebook. Fold two sheets of A4 size, 8 in x 11 in (210 mm x 297 mm) or letter-size paper in half and bind them to a piece of cardboard with a rubber band. Paste some stickers on the book cover to create an original design. You can change the type of paper to colored Kent, natural paper, and others. When you have used up all the pages of your notebook, you can replace them with another set of paper.

The sample notebook shown in this book uses A4 size paper.

To make the Coaster Penholder (on the notebook with pens on it), right, see page 55.

STEP BY STEP

MAKING A RUBBER BAND NOTEBOOK

Materials

- Paper, 15-20 sheets of A4 size, 8 in x 11 in (210 mm x 297 mm) or letter size
- Cardboard, 12.7 in x 8.3 in (322 mm x 210 mm)
- Rubber bands, 3-4 pieces
- Bookbinding tape

Tools

- Scissors
- Craft knife
- Cutting mat
- Pricker
- Ruler

For the Pocket Photo Album
- Colored Kent paper • Rubber band, 1 piece • Bookbinding tape

---

1 Fold five sheets of A4 paper, 8 in x 11 in (210 mm x 297 mm), or letter size paper in half. Make three to four sets.

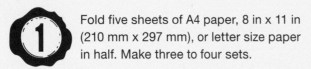

2 Make a book cover using a piece of cardboard. Cut the cardboard in the sizes shown below. Fold the center portion with a gap of 0.5 in (12 mm) width to make the spine of the book cover.

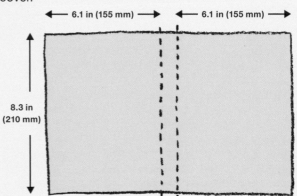

← 6.1 in (155 mm) → ← 6.1 in (155 mm) →

8.3 in (210 mm)

0.5 in (12 mm)

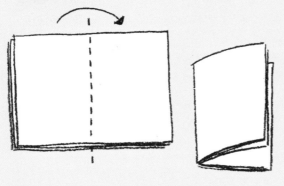

pricker

ruler

3 Place a ruler on the center line of the cardboard and plot guidelines with a pricker. Do not press the pricker too hard.

4 Reinforce the book spine with bookbinding tape.

bookbinding tape

5 Place one set of folded paper on the book cover and bind with a rubber band. Then, bind three to four sets.

book spine

rubber band

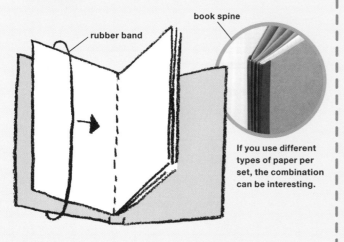

If you use different types of paper per set, the combination can be interesting.

Decorate the book cover with postage stamps and stickers to enhance your design.

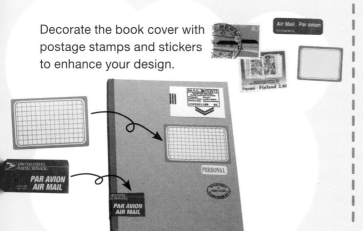

MAKING A RUBBER BAND ALBUM

Use a two-pocket-type photo album that you can get at any photo store. Cut the seams between the top and bottom pockets.

1 Detach the cover of the photo album. Cut the seam between the top and bottom pockets.

2 Make a cover using colored Kent paper to match the size of the photo pocket. Bind the pockets with a rubber band, as you did for the Rubber Band Notebook.

rubber band

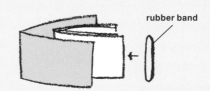

3 If you would like to add more photos, attach another pocket to the cover with rubber bands, then reinforce the spine of the cover with a bookbinding tape.

bookbinding tape

For the Horse-shaped Card Clip shown above,
see page 66.

TRAVELER'S MEMO PAD

When I travel, I spend more time taking down notes than taking pictures. The items shown on these two pages are small memo pads I had used for my travels. If you make a memo pad with a cover of a store's business card or a train ticket, it can reflect the good memories of your past travels, and becomes a handy item for your next trip. A palm-sized memo pad is convenient to carry around. You can make memo pads of various sizes, such as a post card or air ticket size. Why not make a traveler's memo pad decorated with your specially selected cover paper and colored thread for your next trip?

For the Ticket Filing Case shown above right, see page 54.

MAKING A
TRAVELER'S MEMO PAD

Materials

- Train tickets or store business cards (for the cover)
- Memo pad, 40-60 sheets
- Colored drawing paper (for the cover)
- Embroidery threads of varied thickness, about 3.5 times longer than the height of the memo pad, as shown by "A" below diagram

Tools

- Scissors
- Double-sided adhesive tape
- Craft knife
- Cutting mat
- Pricker
- Double clip
- Needle
- Craft glue

1 Prepare a store business card or train ticket you can use for the memo pad cover. Select the paper for the inside pages and bundle them up. Cut the memo pad in the same length as the cover, 0.6 in (15 mm) wider than the store card. Cut out colored drawing paper to match the size of the pad.

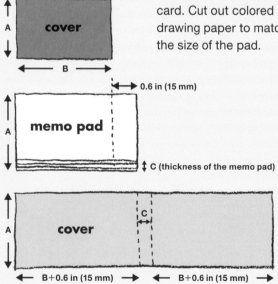

A ↕ | cover | ← B →

← 0.6 in (15 mm)

A ↕ | memo pad | ↕ C (thickness of the memo pad)

A ↕ | cover | C
← B+0.6 in (15 mm) → ← B+0.6 in (15 mm) →

2 Wrap the memo pad with the cover.

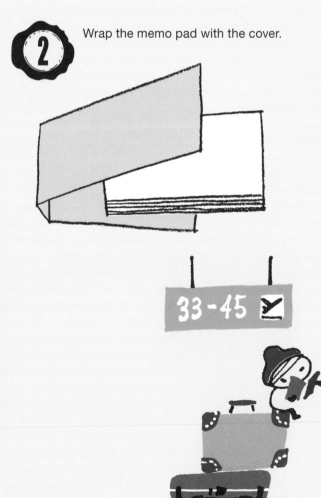

33-45 ✈

3 Affix the memo pad and the cover with a double clip. Place the cover and the memo pad on a cutting mat. Use a pricker to make four holes, about 0.3-0.4 in (8-10 mm) from the edge of the cover spine. Pass an embroidery thread through the holes and bind the cover and the memo pad together, as shown by the drawings in the right column.

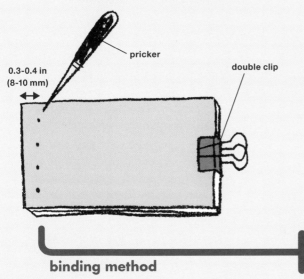

0.3-0.4 in
(8-10 mm)

pricker

double clip

binding method

4 Paste a decorative card or bus/train ticket on the cover using double-sided adhesive tape to finish.

JAPANESE BOOKBINDING STYLE

Bind the memo pad by passing a needle through the center hole, as shown in the drawing below. Paste craft glue on the thread's end and attach it between the pages.

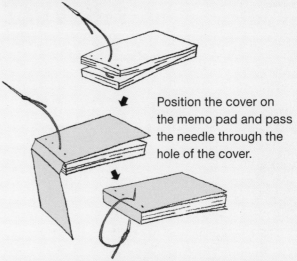

Position the cover on the memo pad and pass the needle through the hole of the cover.

Sew around the cover and the cover spine. The memo pad and cover are now bound together.

Sew the holes as shown in the drawing below.

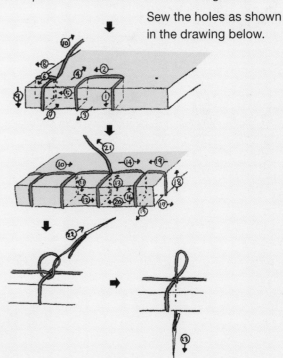

When you have finished binding, tie a knot at the last stitch and sew through the holes, then cut the thread with scissors at the reverse side of the hole.

To make the Magnet
Postage Stamps
shown on the right,
see page 66.

□ 春巻きの皮
□ ミニトマト
□ ちくわ

TEAR-OFF MEMO BOARD

Writing short notes on small pieces of memo paper is more practical than writing them on a large sheet of paper. I made a memo board that allows you to tear off the written portions conveniently. To make this memo board, perforate the memo paper using a pattern wheel, then tear off along the line to pull out your desired size of memo (see photo, left). Try to attach different colored pieces of paper with varied tear-off sizes. When you tear off one portion, a different size and color sheet will appear. Your memo pad will become attractive and fun to use! You can attach the memo board to the refrigerator with a magnet sticker pasted on its back.

To make the Magnet Memo Pad and Magnet Pen and Things-to-do Markers shown on the right, see pages 28 and 66.

MAKING A TEAR-OFF MEMO BOARD

Materials

- Different colored memo paper, B6 size or 5 in x 7 in (128 mm x 182 mm)
- Cardboard (for base), A5 size or 5 in x 8 in (148 mm x 210 mm)
- Cardboard patch, 5.5 in x 1 in (140 mm x 25 mm)
- Patterned fabric, 2.4 in (60 mm) wider and longer than the base cardboard
- Backing (e.g., packaging paper)
- Paper fastener • Bookbinding tape • Magnet sheet

Tools

- Scissors
- Double-sided adhesive tape
- Craft knife
- Pattern wheel
- Cutting mat
- Puncher
- Glue

---

1 Affix double-sided adhesive tape diagonally on the four borders of the cardboard base.

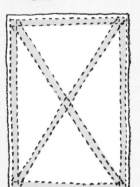

Affix the double-sided tape on the cardboard as marked by dotted lines to hold the cardboard on the fabric.

2 Prepare a piece of fabric, 2.4 in (60 mm) wider and longer than the cardboard. Place the cardboard on the middle of the fabric, leaving about 1.2 in (30 mm) tucked on each side. Fold the four corners of the fabric in triangles, and paste them to the cardboard using glue.

1.2 in (30 mm)

cardboard

fabric

How to make the corners:

Fold the four corners of the fabric inward in triangular shapes, and paste them to the cardboard. Then, turn the shorter sides inward and paste them to the cardboard. Finally, turn the longer sides inward and paste.

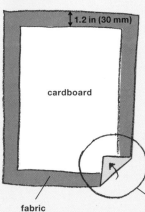

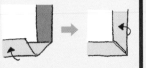

3 Paste the backing (e.g., packaging paper) on the back side of the board made in step 2 using double-sided adhesive tape or glue.

4 Use a pattern wheel to perforate several sheets of memo paper in varied sizes. On the topmost bunched memo sheet, make two holes using a puncher.

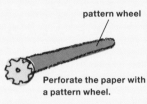

Make two holes using a puncher.

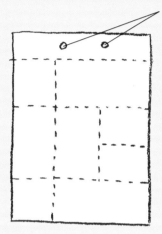

pattern wheel

Perforate the paper with a pattern wheel.

If you use different colored sheets, you will enjoy seeing the changes in color as you tear off one memo after another.

5 Use a craft knife to make two slits on the cardboard and insert a paper fastener from the back side. Affix the back of the paper fastener with bookbinding tape.

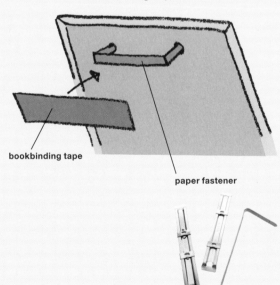

bookbinding tape

paper fastener

6 Prepare a cardboard patch, 5.5 in x 1 in (140 mm x 25 mm) as reinforcement. Make two holes on it using a puncher. Place the memo pad on the cardboard, then the patch, and file with the fastener cover.

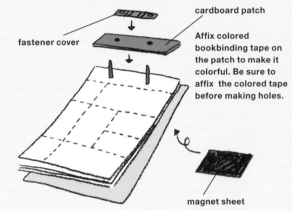

fastener cover

cardboard patch

Affix colored bookbinding tape on the patch to make it colorful. Be sure to affix the colored tape before making holes.

magnet sheet

7 Paste an appropriate sized magnet sheet on the back of the memo board. The memo board can be attached to the refrigerator or a white board.

MINI MESSAGE CARD TAGS

These mini message cards are made from binded small card tags. They can be used to send out short messages. The tag shape looks impressive.

Remove the ring from the binded card tags to use the cards individually. Cut the top two corners of the card. Attach an eyelet on the card using an eyelet puncher. Pass a piece of string through the hole.

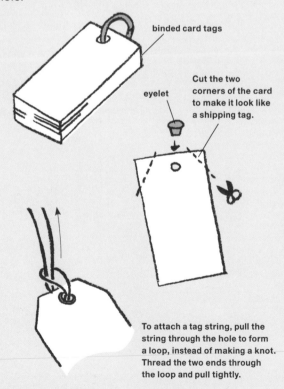

binded card tags

eyelet

Cut the two corners of the card to make it look like a shipping tag.

To attach a tag string, pull the string through the hole to form a loop, instead of making a knot. Thread the two ends through the loop and pull tightly.

MAGNET MEMO PAD AND MAGNET PEN

Attach a magnet on a memo pad or a pen to stick it on the refrigerator or a whiteboard.

Attach a strip of magnet sheet on the back of a memo pad or on the barrel of a pen using a double-sided adhesive tape. If you already have a magnet sticker, stick the magnet directly on the pad and pen.

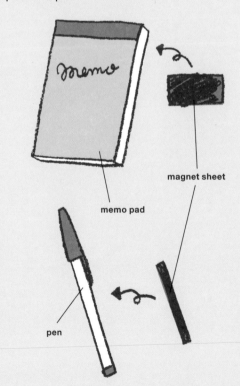

memo

magnet sheet

memo pad

pen

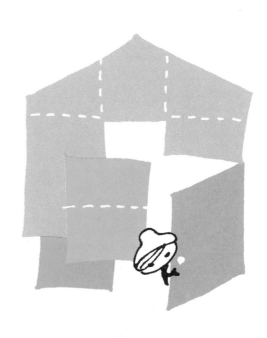

How I Customize My Diaries

This is the diary I used during my school days.
When I had no extra space to write on,
I attached a notebook to the diary,
creating a book within a book.

The diary was the first item I started to customize to meet my needs. I have kept my diaries from my high school days and they surround me with many memories.

When I was in high school, I posted various items in my diary, such as clippings from recruiting magazines, store maps, movie schedules, candy wrappers, and so on. These items filled up my customized diaries. Usually, I wrote directly in my diary, but when I had no more space to write, I had to paste sticky notes on the pages to add more writing space.

Several years later, I learned to use paper clips for many purposes. I attached a clear plastic pocket to my diary using a paper clip and decorated it with postage stamps. In the past, I used a thin, monthly type diary because I wanted to look at everything at one glance. When I used to work in an office, I used a weekly or a ring file type of diary. My diaries are simple to make and I always enjoy customizing them.

I have two indispensable items for customizing my diaries: a things-to-do list and a checklist. The things-to-do list is a list of things to do for the day. It is an itemized reminder. You can find diaries with things-to-do lists in stores. In my customized diary, I draw square boxes and list up things to do. When I finish doing one item, I check the box in the list.

I list up the names of people whom I have to send an email to on that day, and check the corresponding boxes when I have finished sending the email. My devise is an improvised things-to-do list with check mark boxes. If the items are listed in chronological order, I can

quickly grasp which item to do first. I like this list because I feel a sense of achievement when I have finished one task in the list by checking each box one by one.

When I looked through my diaries over the past twenty years, I found a business card of a store I frequently visited long time ago. Then, I remembered what I did at that time. I felt as though I was caught in a time warp—that a certain period of time in my life has been condensed in each of my diaries.

Coffee Filter Pocket as shown in the Easy-to-make Stationery Items section on page 55. It is a practical supplement for my diary.

CHAPTER 2
FILES,
FOLDERS,
AND CASES

MONTHLY FILE ENVELOPE CASE

One day, I decided to make a monthly file similar to the one I found at a store when I traveled abroad. I simply attached twelve envelopes to represent the twelve months. Now, I use this file to organize business cards, movie tickets, receipts, and more. If you attach index tags on the envelopes, it becomes more convenient for sorting small items. You can also change the size of the envelopes to fit your needs. If you use colored envelopes, you can create a pretty business-like file organizer.

To make the Ticket Filing Case shown above, left, see page 54.

STEP BY STEP

MAKING A MONTHLY FILE ENVELOPE CASE

Materials
- **Envelopes, 12**   • **Colored Kent paper**
- **Velcro tape**   • **Bookbinding tape**

Tools
- **Scissors**
- **Craft knife**
- **Cutting mat**
- **Double-sided adhesive tape**
- **Pricker**

Attach an index tag on the top edge of each envelope to make it useful for sorting out items.

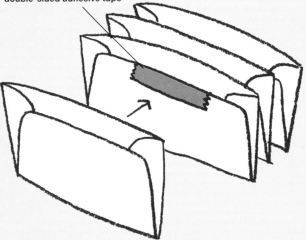

1 Take out twelve envelopes, and cut off the flaps.

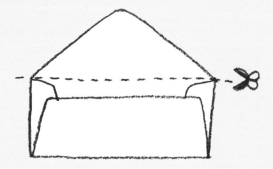

2 Affix a double-sided adhesive tape at the center of the top edge of each envelope, and stick the envelopes together.

double-sided adhesive tape

If you affix the tape from one end to the other end of the envelope, the envelope will not open wide enough. The length of the tape should be half of the width of the envelope.

3 To make the file cover, cut colored Kent paper as shown below.
· A: height of the envelope
· B: height of the rear side of the envelope
· C: thickness of the twelve envelopes
Use a pricker to plot guidelines on the envelopes, as shown on the right. To fold the flap, mark guidelines so that the flap can be folded easily.

Use colored envelopes for a more striking appearance.

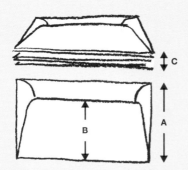

C

B

A

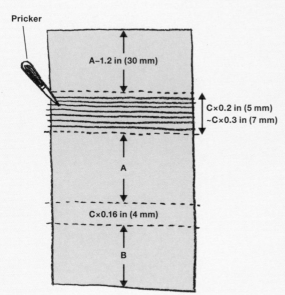

Pricker

A−1.2 in (30 mm)

C×0.2 in (5 mm) ~C×0.3 in (7 mm)

A

C×0.16 in (4 mm)

B

4 Attach the set of envelopes to the file cover made in step 3 using double-sided adhesive tape. Affix Velcro tape at the back of the flap, and on the other side of the cover.

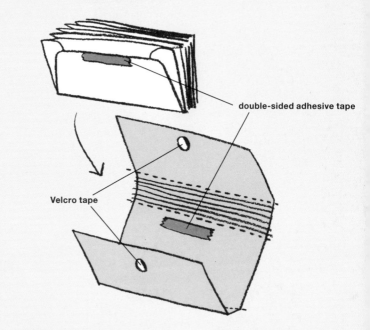

double-sided adhesive tape

Velcro tape

5 Tape the edge of the flap with bookbinding tape to reinforce it. You can use a matching colored tape for a design accent.

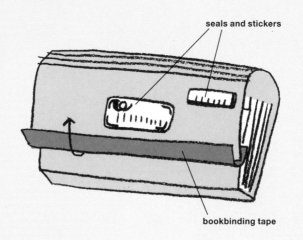

seals and stickers

bookbinding tape

To make the Wrapping Paper Aerogram shown
below, right, see page 87.

CARD-SIZE FOLDER

This is a mini folder that is convenient for carrying small items, like postage stamps and store cards. It can be made quickly by pasting fabric, cardboard, and bookbinding tape together. You can attach a money clip to the card folder to hold receipts, and a card file to keep store cards. Enjoy making your personalized card-size folder! The point in making a charming folder is to match the colors of the fabric and bookbinding tape wisely.

To make the Photo Case shown above, right, see page 54.

MAKING A CARD-SIZE FOLDER

Materials

- **Patterned fabric**
- **Cardboard**
- **Backing**
- **Large rubber band, 0.2 in (6 mm) wide**
- **Bookbinding tape**
- **Paper fastener**
- **Label seal**
- **Card file**
- **Money clip** • **Double clip**

Tools

- **Scissors**
- **Double-sided adhesive tape**
- **Craft knife**
- **Cutting mat**

---

1 Prepare a piece of cardboard, 3 in (70 mm) W x 4 in (100 mm) L. Use double-sided adhesive tape to paste the cardboard to the fabric, which should be 2 in (40 mm) wider and longer than the cardboard. Fold and paste the four corners of the fabric to the cardboard with glue.

2 Paste the backing paper to the reverse side of the cardboard using a glue tape or double-sided adhesive tape. Make two sets of this panel.

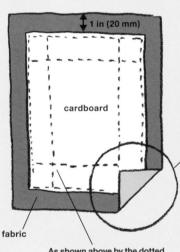

1 in (20 mm)

cardboard

fabric

As shown above by the dotted lines, affix double-sided adhesive tape on the cardboard and paste the cardboard to the fabric.

How to make the corners:

Fold the four corners of the fabric inward in triangular shapes, and paste them to the cardboard. Then, turn the shorter sides inward and paste them to the cardboard. Finally, turn the longer sides inward and paste.

3 Position the two panels made in steps 1 and 2, making sure they are 0.2 in (6 mm) apart. Connect the two panels by wrapping a bookbinding tape around them, leaving 0.2 in (6 mm) between the panels. Affix the tape firmly.

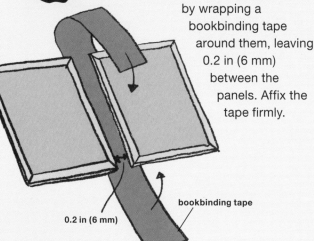

0.2 in (6 mm)

bookbinding tape

4 Make two parallel slits on the panel, measuring 0.6 in (15 mm) inside from the edge of the panel. The two slits should be about 0.1 in (3 mm) apart.

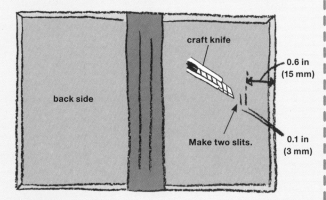

back side

craft knife

0.6 in (15 mm)

Make two slits.

0.1 in (3 mm)

5 Put a rubber band around the panel made in step 4.

front side

rubber band

6 Fasten a paper fastener to the panel, holding the rubber band by the legs of the fastener.

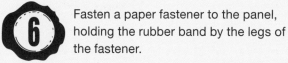

legs of the paper fastener

7 Turn up the legs of the paper fastener on the back of the panel. Paste a label seal to cover up the legs.

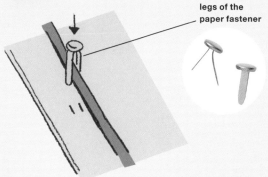

label seal

8 Attach a card file using a double clip, or insert a money clip to the panel for filing items.

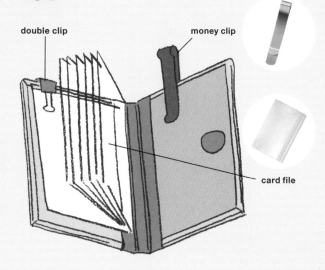

double clip

money clip

card file

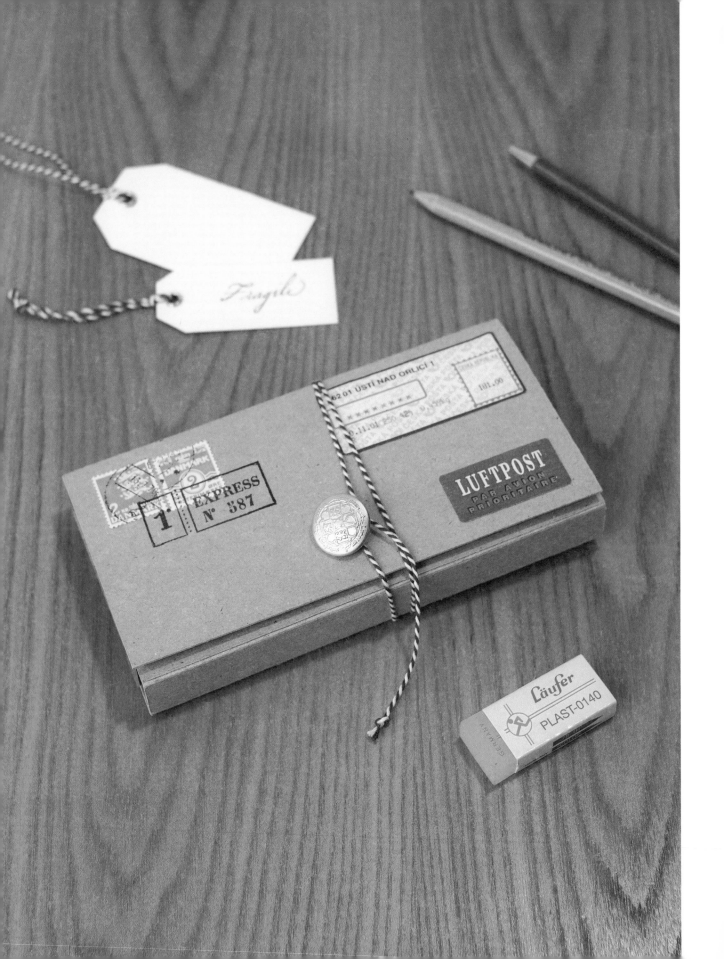

PEN CASE BOX

I always carry my pen case with me, so it easily wears out. To replace it, I thought of making a practical pen case similar to the one I used when I was little. You can make it by just folding a piece of cardboard and tying a piece of string around it. You can even make a tool box in the same way. Since the pen case is made of plain material, you can decorate the surface freely. The pen case box shown here is designed to look like a parcel post from a foreign country. It has a unique style.

To make the Mini Message Cards shown in the top left corner of the left photo, see page 28.

MAKING A
PEN CASE BOX

Materials

- Paper box, large enough to contain pencils (e.g., cookie box)
- Cardboard
- Rubber band, 0.4 in (10 mm) wide
- Button
- Wire
- String or narrow ribbon

Tools

- Double-sided adhesive tape
- Adhesive (cellophane) tape
- Scissors
- Craft knife
- Cutting mat
- Pricker
- Pencil
- Ruler

---

1 Find a suitable box to contain pencils. Cut the cardboard, following the dimensions shown below.

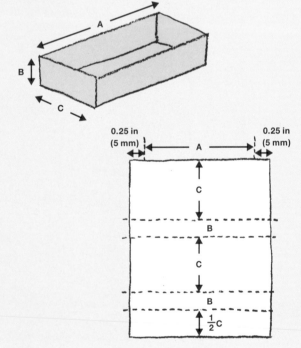

2 Place the box at the center of the cardboard, then use a pencil to plot guidelines around the three sides of the box, as shown below.

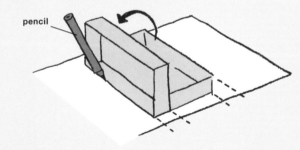

3 Use a ruler and a pricker to plot guidelines on the cardboard, following the traced lines in step 2.

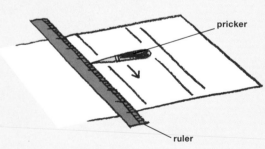

4 Affix two pieces of double-sided adhesive tape on the cardboard (inside the traced lines), as shown below. Place the box over the tape, then fold the cardboard over the box.

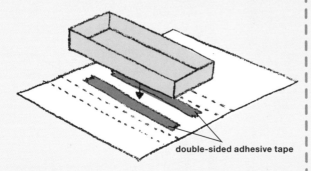

double-sided adhesive tape

5 Attach the narrower side of the cardboard to the top edge of the box using a wide rubber band.

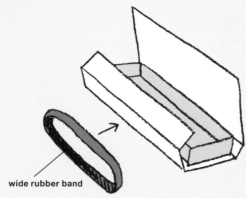

wide rubber band

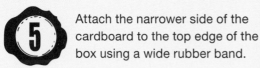

6 Punch a hole on the wider side of the cardboard using a pricker. Thread a piece of wire through a button and twist the two ends. then insert the wire into the hole. Unwind the wire on the back side of the lid and affix the wire with adhesive cellophane tape.

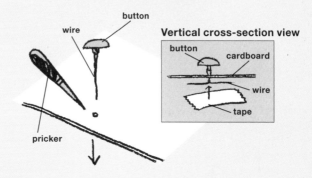

wire
button
pricker

Vertical cross-section view

button
cardboard
wire
tape

7 Tie a piece of string or ribbon around the button, and wrap the box with it so that the box lid will not open loosely. The length of the string may be about two-fold of the perimeter of the box, enough to wrap around the box and close at the button.

string

Decorate the top side with postage stamps or seals of foreign countries.

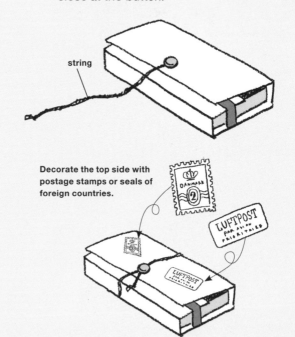

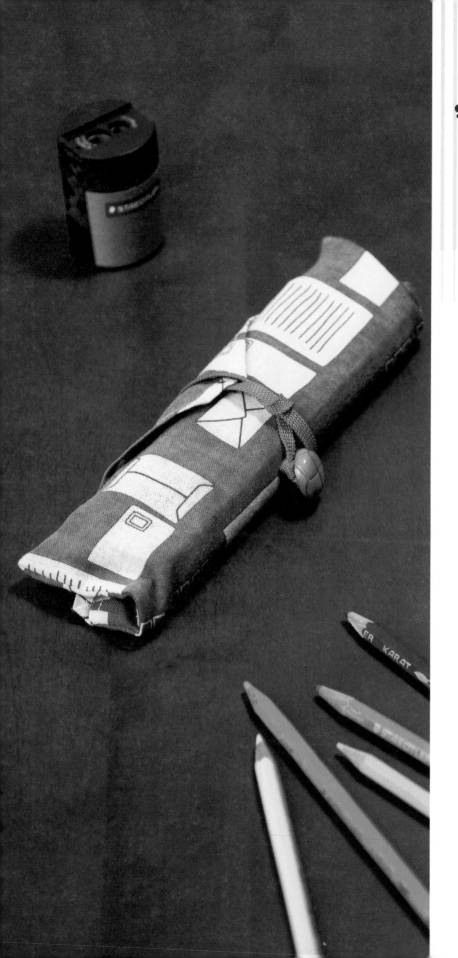

FACE CLOTH (TENUGUI) PENCIL CASE

Handmade

If you have an extra *tenugui* or cotton face cloth in your home, you can design a pencil case with it. Since the material is made of soft cotton, you can easily adjust the size of the pencil case according to the volume of your contents. You can expand or fold it, and the cloth is washable; hence, you do not have to buy a new patterned fabric. Use your face cloth in your home and create your original pencil case. The fabric can also be replaced with a handkerchief.

MAKING A FACE CLOTH (TENUGUI) PENCIL CASE

Materials
- **Face cloth**
- **Ribbon, 0.2 in (6 mm) W x 11 in (280 mm) L**
- **Button**

Tools
- **Scissors**
- **Sewing machine**
- **Thread**
- **Needle**
- **Double-sided adhesive tape**

① Cut the face cloth as shown.

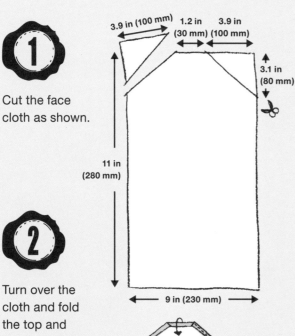

3.9 in (100 mm) 1.2 in (30 mm) 3.9 in (100 mm)

3.1 in (80 mm)

11 in (280 mm)

9 in (230 mm)

② Turn over the cloth and fold the top and bottom edges inside by 0.3 in (7 mm). Hold the seams together with double-sided adhesive tape and sew with the sewing machine.

back side

0.3 in (7 mm)

double-sided adhesive tape

③ Fold the fabric upward, 3.9 in (100 mm) from the bottom edge. Sew the right and left edges, 0.2 in (5 mm) with the sewing machine. Then, turn the fabric inside out.

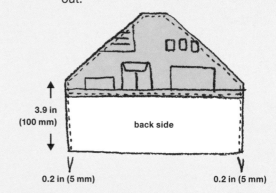

3.9 in (100 mm)

back side

0.2 in (5 mm)   0.2 in (5 mm)

④ Tie a button to the end of the ribbon and attach the ribbon on the triangular flap with a needle and thread.

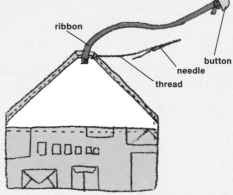

ribbon

needle

button

thread

⑤ Put pencils or other writing items in the pencil case and tie the ribbon around the pencil case to close the flap in place.

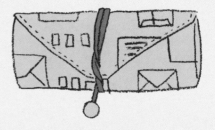

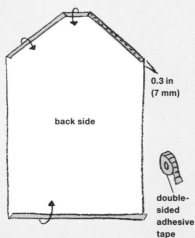

To make the Envelope Calendar shown on the top left corner, see page 67.

TOTE BOOK

Using an attractive piece of fabric, I made a book cover in the shape of a tote bag to carry pocket books. The design concept behind this tote book is that you can take it with you when you go for a walk, or use it to hold a pocket book and coins. You can carry the tote book anywhere you go—café or park—just open the cover and read your book. Decorate the book cover with your favorite key holders or pin badges to make it look like a real tote bag. Make a nice tote book only for your special books.

To make the Message Tag hung on the green and white tote book shown on the left page, see page 86.

MAKING A TOTE BOOK

Materials
• Piece of fabric   • Ribbon

Tools
• Scissors
• Double-sided adhesive tape
• Sewing machine
• Embroidery thread
• Needle

1 Prepare a piece of fabric and cut it as shown in the diagram below. Turn both sides of the fabric inward.

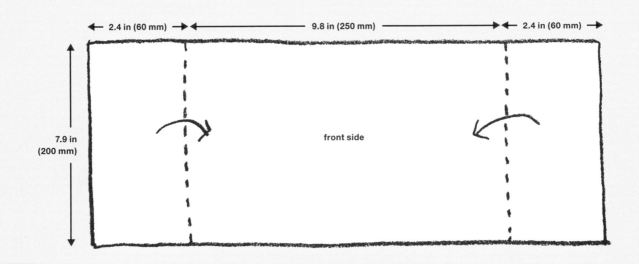

← 2.4 in (60 mm) →   ← 9.8 in (250 mm) →   ← 2.4 in (60 mm) →

7.9 in
(200 mm)

front side

Sew the top and bottom hems, 0.6 in (15 mm) with a sewing machine. Then, turn the fabric inside out and sew about 0.1 in (2 mm) from the top and bottom edges.

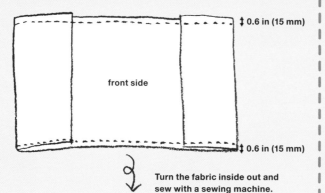

↕ 0.6 in (15 mm)

front side

↕ 0.6 in (15 mm)

Turn the fabric inside out and sew with a sewing machine.

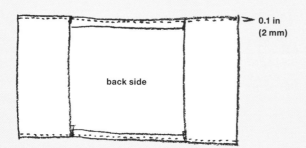

→ 0.1 in (2 mm)

back side

Prepare two pieces of ribbons to make the handles: 0.4 in (10 mm) x 9.4 in (240 mm). Attach the ribbon handles on the cover with a 1.6 in (40 mm) piece of double-sided tape. Stitch the center line of the handles with a needle and thickly stranded embroidery thread.

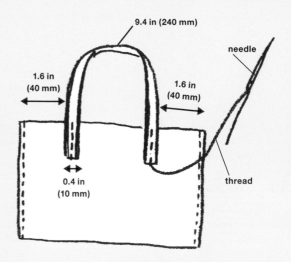

9.4 in (240 mm)

1.6 in (40 mm)

1.6 in (40 mm)

needle

thread

0.4 in (10 mm)

Attach your favorite pin badges or key holders. The tote book will look like a real bag.

ASSORTED BUS AND TRAIN PASS CASES

Since I could not find any ready-made bus and train pass cases that I wanted to use, I decided to make my own. I started making them with small envelopes or paper that featured pretty designs.

Now, I'm always making many bus and train pass cases with available unique materials. Sometimes, I use them as card files organized by group. My bus and train pass cases have semicircle notches on the top edge, so that you can easily pull a card in and out from the notch opening. These bus and train pass cases are also suitable for other cards of the same size.

MAKING ASSORTED BUS AND TRAIN PASS CASES

Materials
- **Paper (or envelopes and thin, sturdy paper, like bank transfer forms)**
- **Bookbinding tape**

Tools
- **Scissors**
- **Embroidery thread**
- **Needle**

STEP BY STEP

Single Case

← 3.9 in (100 mm) →

4.7 in (120 mm)

Cut out a piece of paper as shown in the diagram. Fold it in half.

Paste the left and right edges of the paper using a bookbinding tape.

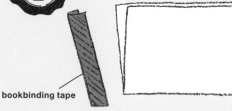

bookbinding tape

To make semicircle notches on the top edge of the case, cut the top and bottom edges of the paper in a semicircle pattern, as shown in the right diagram. The notch is designed so one can push the card out easily from the bottom of the case.

Double Case

Just like the single case, cut out a piece of paper, 4.7 in (120 mm) x 7.5 in (190 mm). Fold it in half.

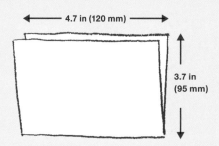

← 4.7 in (120 mm) →

3.7 in (95 mm)

1. Paste the left and right edges of the paper with a bookbinding tape.
2. Stitch the center line with a piece of thread and needle.
3. Make four semi-lunar notches on the top and bottom edges of the paper.

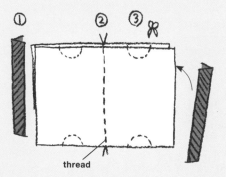

thread

Fold the paper in half.

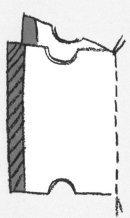

TICKET FILING CASE

This ticket filing case holds concert, movie, and other tickets. You can easily make it using an old envelope, and discard it after use.

Cut an envelope and the filing case is done. Use envelopes of utility bills that have a pattern inside to hide the contents.

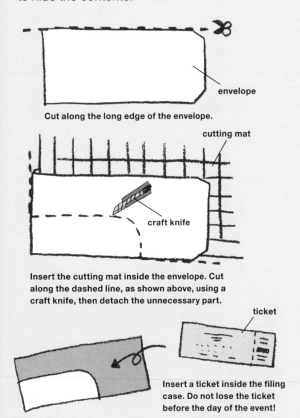

envelope

Cut along the long edge of the envelope.

cutting mat

craft knife

Insert the cutting mat inside the envelope. Cut along the dashed line, as shown above, using a craft knife, then detach the unnecessary part.

ticket

Insert a ticket inside the filing case. Do not lose the ticket before the day of the event!

PHOTO CASE

When you give your friends pictures as a gift, you may want to use a special photo case rather than an ordinary envelope to make your gift presentation more attractive. Make a photo case to fit the size of your picture.

Cut a piece of cardboard in the size shown in the diagram below. Mark the lines to be folded using a pricker, as indicated by the dotted lines. Then, fold the marked lines.

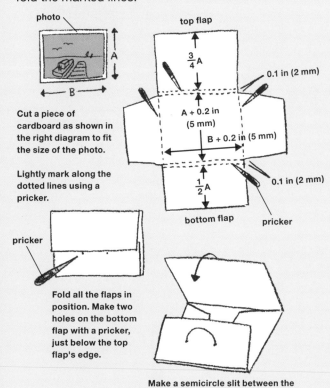

photo

top flap

$\frac{3}{4}$A

0.1 in (2 mm)

A + 0.2 in (5 mm)

B + 0.2 in (5 mm)

$\frac{1}{2}$A

0.1 in (2 mm)

bottom flap

pricker

Cut a piece of cardboard as shown in the right diagram to fit the size of the photo.

Lightly mark along the dotted lines using a pricker.

pricker

Fold all the flaps in position. Make two holes on the bottom flap with a pricker, just below the top flap's edge.

Make a semicircle slit between the two holes to insert the top flap.

COASTER PENHOLDER

This penholder is made from a coaster and an elastic band. You can carry it looped around your notebook or memo pad, so you do not need to have a pencil case.

Affix bookbinding tape, for reinforcement, on the back of a paper coaster. Cut slots on the coaster with a craft knife. Weave an elastic band through the slits. Join the elastic band ends with an elastic band connecter to make a loop.

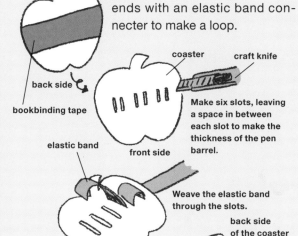

back side

bookbinding tape

coaster

craft knife

Make six slots, leaving a space in between each slot to make the thickness of the pen barrel.

front side

elastic band

Weave the elastic band through the slots.

back side of the coaster

This elastic band connecter comes in two parts, which joins the elastic band ends.

Join the elastic band ends with the band connecter.

COFFEE FILTER POCKET

It is useful to have a coffee filter pocket at the back of a notebook cover. It also looks charming.

Paste a coffee filter on the back of a notebook cover using double-sided adhesive tape.

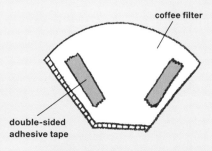

coffee filter

double-sided adhesive tape

Affix the double stick tape on the filter, leaving some space on the right and left edges to open the pocket widely.

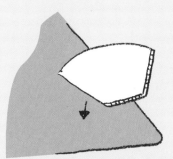

Paste the coffee filter on the notebook cover to finish.

Travel Notebooks
and Plastic Zip Bags

When I travel, I keep my travel memorabilia in a notebook. Rather than using one kind of notebook, I make different kinds for each trip and decorate the covers with seals, illustrations, or characters that would remind me of the country or the city I visited, such as New York, San Francisco, Paris, Hong Kong, and others.

I keep restaurant maps and tickets of museums, movies, and musicals I have been to instantly in my notebook, rather than filing them in a scrap book later. That way before I return to Japan I have finished compiling my travel notebooks.

When I go on a short trip and find no need to make a notebook, I keep my travel memorabilia in a plastic zip bag. I organize my travel souvenirs by country. When a friend plans to go to a country that I have visited before, I lend him/her my travel zip bag. My travel notebooks and zip bags have become very useful travel guides.

CHAPTER 3
SMALL
STATIONERY
ITEMS

WIRE BOOKMARKS

These wire bookmarks look like flowers blooming from a book.
It is important to select a suitable button carefully.

RIBBON BOOKMARKS

The ribbons can be seen from both the top and tail edges of a book.
Aren't they cute? You can make several kinds with different widths.

PAPER CLIP BOOKMARKS

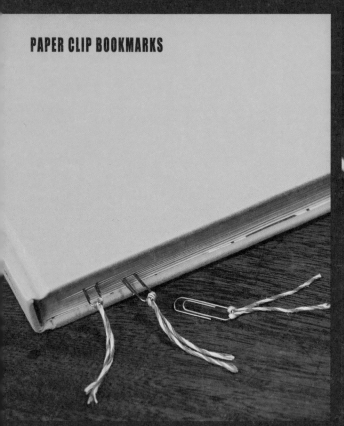

These paper clip bookmaks are simple and they
firmly hold the top edge of a page.

WOODEN BOOKMARKS

These wooden bookmarks are like
sticky notes that you can use for any purpose.

ASSORTED BOOKMARKS

Make bookmarks that will make your reading time more enjoyable. Depending on your chosen materials and your ideas, you can enjoy making various types of bookmarks. The items shown here are made of buttons threaded with wire, ice-cream spoons stamped with rubber stamps, and envelope corners. These bookmarks are designed not only to accompany your books, but also to create a relaxed atmosphere for your home library. The more bookmarks you make, the more books you will end up reading!

ENVELOPE CORNER BOOKMARKS
You can create animal motifs and other patterns. They are truly charming!

STEP BY STEP

MAKING ASSORTED BOOKMARKS

WIRE BOOKMARKS

Materials
- Buttons
- Paper
- Wire

Tools
- Pricker
- Scissors

1 Pass a fine piece of wire through the holes of a button. If the button has four holes, pass the wire diagonally.

For a flower motif button, make a leaf with green paper. Make a hole in the leaf with a pricker, and thread the wire closely to the bottom of the button.

wire

button

green paper leaf

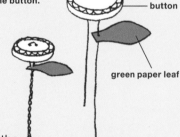

2 Twist the wire from the bottom of the button.

Make a green leaf as shown in the photo.

RIBBON BOOKMARKS

Materials
- Ribbon
- Charm pendant

Tools
- Thread
- Needle

1 Fold the ends of the ribbon twice. Stitch the folded end with a single stitch. Make four to five stitches.

Fold the ribbon ends twice.

needle

Stitch with a single stitch from end to end.

thread

2 Sew a charm pendant on the stitched ribbon end.

charm pendant

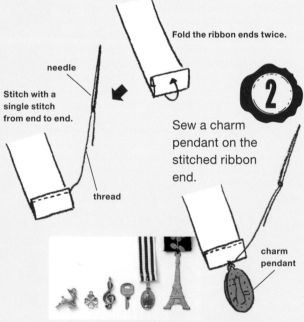

assorted charm pendants

PAPER CLIP BOOKMARKS

Materials
- Paper clips (gem clips)
- String

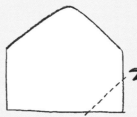

Tie a piece of string to a paper clip.

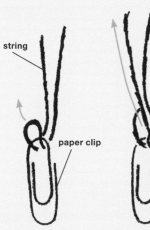  

string

paper clip

a. Fold the string in half and pass through the leg of the paper clip.

b. Pass the two ends of the string through the hole of the string.

c. Pull the string to fasten it to the paper clip.

ENVELOPE CORNER BOOKMARKS

Materials
- Used envelopes

Tools
- Craft knife
- Scissors
- Cutting mat

Use the template shown on the end of this book or make a copy of the template.

Use scissors to cut the corner of a used envelope, making a triangular shape. **1**

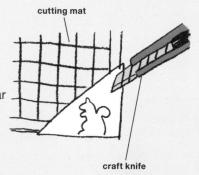

cutting mat

craft knife

Draw an animal shape on the triangular corner. Insert the triangular paper into the corner of a cutting mat. Use a craft knife to cut out the animal shape. **2**

Unfold the animal shape that you cut with a craft knife into an upright position. The work is finished. **3**

WOODEN BOOKMARKS

Materials
- Wooden spoons or popsicle sticks

Tools
- Rubber stamps

Decorate a wooden spoon or ice cream spoon with a rubber stamp.

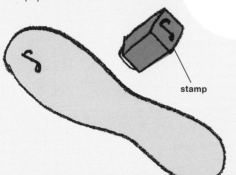

stamp

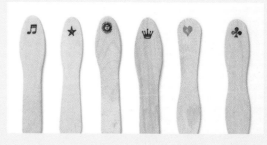

Enjoy stamping various stamp designs on the wooden bookmarks!

PAPER CLIP HOLDERS

I made paper clip holders from spools and cardboard, and just pasted a plain magnet sheet around them. They look functional and decorative. The hedgehog motif fits perfectly for the paper clip holder since paper clips look like the spines of the hedgehog. Birds and porcupine fish also make interesting motifs. When you roll the spool paper clip holder, you can quickly collect the paper clips scattered on the desk. The design is simple and efficient.

MAKING PAPER CLIP HOLDERS

Materials
- Magnet sheet (adhesive type)
- Cardboard   • Spool

Tools
- Scissors   • Double-sided adhesive tape
- Craft knife   • Cutting mat

See the end of this book for the template of the hedgehog.

You can cut it out or make a photocopy.

STEP BY STEP

HEDGEHOG PAPER CLIP HOLDER

1 Cut a piece of cardboard in the sizes shown in the right diagram. Mark two lines for folding using a pricker.

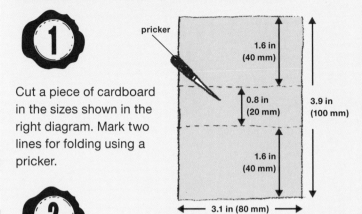

pricker

1.6 in (40 mm)

0.8 in (20 mm)

3.9 in (100 mm)

1.6 in (40 mm)

3.1 in (80 mm)

2 Take out two adhesive magnet sheets, 2.6 in x 1.6 in (65 mm x 40 mm). Paste them on the cardboard.

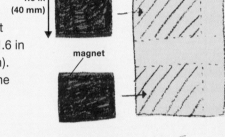

2.6 in (65 mm)

1.6 in (40 mm)

magnet

3 After pasting the magnet sheets, cut the cardboard. You can cut randomly or use the template found at the end of this book.

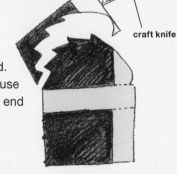

craft knife

4 As shown in the diagram, fold the cardboard so the magnet is facing outside and glue the inner sides of the hedgehog with double-sided adhesive tape. Paint the face of the hedgehog to finish.

double-sided adhesive tape

SPOOL PAPER CLIP HOLDER

1 Prepare a spool with a thick barrel.

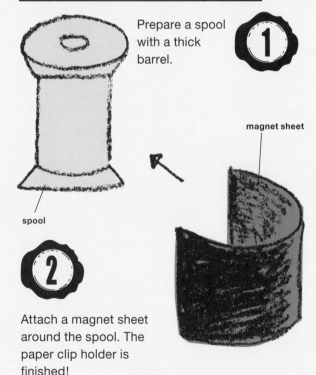

magnet sheet

spool

2 Attach a magnet sheet around the spool. The paper clip holder is finished!

THINGS-TO-DO MARKERS

These clip markers help you to quickly find your priority items.

Cut a piece of paper using a template, as shown at the end of this book. Paste the paper on a wooden clothespin.

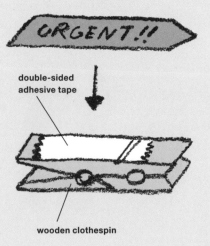

ORGENT!!

double-sided adhesive tape

wooden clothespin

MAGNET POSTAGE STAMPS

These postage stamps are simply made from a magnet sheet backing. Using varied foreign stamps will create a pretty effect.

Paste a postage stamp on a magnet sheet using double-sided adhesive tape. Cut out the magnet sheet along the edge of the stamp using a craft knife.

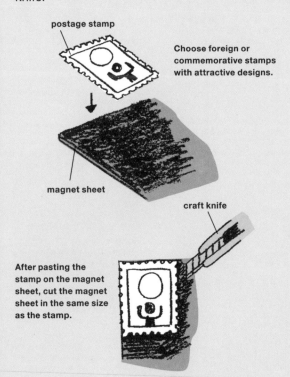

postage stamp

Choose foreign or commemorative stamps with attractive designs.

magnet sheet

craft knife

After pasting the stamp on the magnet sheet, cut the magnet sheet in the same size as the stamp.

ENVELOPE CALENDAR

This envelope calendar is made from a large office envelope cut in custom size. It can be hung on the wall and used as an organizer for direct mail or monthly receipts.

Use a large A4-sized office envelope, 8.3 in x 11.7 in (210 mm x 297 mm) or letter size that has an accordion gusset. Cut the envelope in the size shown in the diagram below. Paste a calendar on the front side of the envelope.

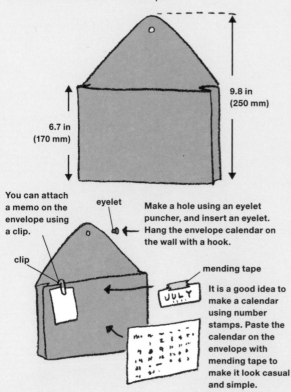

9.8 in (250 mm)

6.7 in (170 mm)

You can attach a memo on the envelope using a clip.

clip

eyelet

Make a hole using an eyelet puncher, and insert an eyelet. Hang the envelope calendar on the wall with a hook.

mending tape

It is a good idea to make a calendar using number stamps. Paste the calendar on the envelope with mending tape to make it look casual and simple.

HORSE-SHAPED CARD CLIP

This charming card holder shows the traditional Swedish Dala Häst horse motif. It can also be used as a desk ornament.

Cut out a Dala Häst horse pattern from a piece of colored drawing paper using a template, as shown at the end of this book. Paste wooden clothespins on the paper using a double stick tape to finish. You can stick tiny round label seals on the horse.

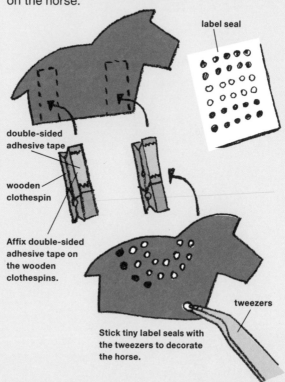

label seal

double-sided adhesive tape

wooden clothespin

Affix double-sided adhesive tape on the wooden clothespins.

tweezers

Stick tiny label seals with the tweezers to decorate the horse.

Supermarket Products and Stationery Items

When I travel abroad, I love to look around supermarkets, stationery shops, and home centers. You can find many practical, functional, and attractive products for everyday use in these establishments.

I often encounter products that I do not know how to use. For example, I bought a coned measuring cup and a container for diluting paint. I was not sure how to use them, but now I use them as a clip container and a pencil holder, respectively, in my work.

I always look for gum tape and sticky notes in stationery stores, which come in a wide range of designs and colors that are not readily available in Japan. I find these products irresistible because I use them frequently.

As a designer, I am very interested in packages that have hooks or headers. I am happy just to look at those items in the window display.

CHAPTER 4
DECORATIVE
GIFT
ITEMS

ASSORTED LETTER FORMATS
SENDING OUT LETTERS IN DIFFERENT FORMS

SEVEN ASSORTED LETTER STYLES

I prepared various objects to find out if they can be sent out by mail from Japan:

1. First, I tried to send out a herb candy package because I found the packaging cute. I mailed it as an irregularly sized mail with the address label pasted on it.

2. Next, I sent out an imported salt container. I rolled up a letter and pushed it into the container. Since it was too bulky to drop in the mailbox, I went to the post office to have it delivered.

3. I also sent out a Camembert cheese package. I sealed the container tightly and attached an address seal on it.

4. I tried to send out a plastic liquor bottle made in Korea. Since it was made of plastic, I thought it would not break. It was also sent out as ordinary mail.

5. I was able to send out a fabric pouch as a letter. The pouch itself was no problem but the postal clerk advised me to adjust the loose ends of the string attached to the pouch.

6. Once I was in a grocery and I spotted a gumbo package, then I got an idea of using it as an air cushion bag to make an envelope. I stapled a piece of paper on the cushion bag and wrote the address on it.

7. Lastly, I used a luggage tag that had a small envelope attached to it. I received it when I took a long distance bus ride in Canada. I was able send it out as an ordinary letter.

1

2

3

4

Once, I received a Japanese kokeshi doll as a letter from my friend who lived in Sendai.
The kokeshi doll had a letter inside it, and the address label was pasted on the body.
It was delivered to my home with an ordinary postage stamp on it.
I was surprised to know that such an item could be mailed as a letter.
I got so excited that I immediately bought a dozen kokeshi dolls.
Since then, I have tried to send out letters in various forms.
Find out from your local post office if you are able to send out the following objects as letters.

5

6

7

PLEASURE OF SENDING AND RECEIVING LETTERS

Once, I tried sending out letters in various styles and materials, I realized that it was so much fun to think about creating unique styles of letters, and how much the recipient would be surprised to receive them. I imagine the recipient's joy in the same way I would be thrilled to receive such an unusual and interesting letter. I also enjoyed conversing with the postal clerk, and learning that almost any item can be sent out by post. Now I feel like sending a different form of letter each time I write to someone. Letters look more attractive if they are specially designed by season or shape using appropriate seasonal or illustrative postage stamps. Why don't you try to send out unique letters from now on?

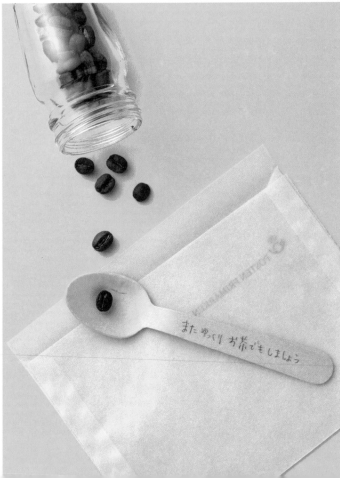

GREETING CARDS

We send out greeting cards to convey Christmas greetings, congratulatory messages, and other occasional wishes. If you make greeting cards of various shapes, your message can become more meaningful. Try making cute greeting cards now!

MAKING GREETING CARDS

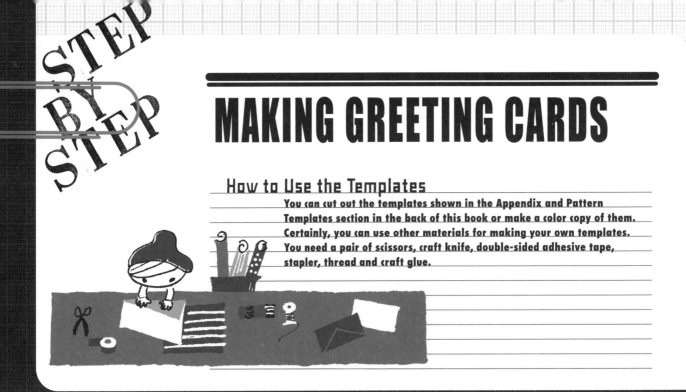

How to Use the Templates

You can cut out the templates shown in the Appendix and Pattern Templates section in the back of this book or make a color copy of them. Certainly, you can use other materials for making your own templates. You need a pair of scissors, craft knife, double-sided adhesive tape, stapler, thread and craft glue.

ANIMAL POSTMAN: BEAR, DOVE

These sample animal and bird motifs can be used for any occasion, such as Christmas or events to express congratulations. They are designed as though the animal or bird is delivering the message.

Draw a picture of an animal on a sheet of drawing paper. Cut along the arm (in the case of the bear motif) or the legs (in the case of the dove) as shown by the dotted lines.

Cut the red lines, as shown above.

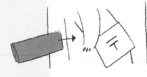

Roll up your message sheet and insert it through the slits.

BUTTERFLY

This butterfly-shaped greeting card shows the image of a butterfly flying over the fields in springtime.

Use several pieces of paper, such as tracing paper or colored paper. Fold a piece of paper in half and cut out a shape of a butterfly's wings and antennas. Fold two pieces of paper and cut out another butterfly wing shape, but without antennas.

one sheet of butterfly wings with antennas

two sheets of butterfly wings without antennas

message

Place the two sheets of wings with no antennas on the sheet with antennas. Staple them together in the center of the wings.

stapler

LAUNDRY

This card motif shows the image of summer—laundry on a clothesline swings with the breeze under the sun. Turn over the T-shirt-shaped paper and write your message.

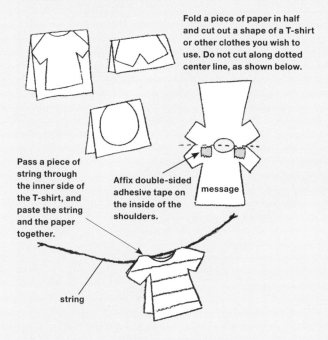

Fold a piece of paper in half and cut out a shape of a T-shirt or other clothes you wish to use. Do not cut along dotted center line, as shown below.

Affix double-sided adhesive tape on the inside of the shoulders.

message

Pass a piece of string through the inner side of the T-shirt, and paste the string and the paper together.

string

COFFEE

This card has a real coffee bean attached to it, which gives off the fragrance of coffee.

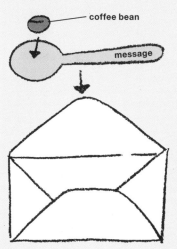

coffee bean

message

Paste a real coffee bean on a wooden spoon using craft glue. Write down your message on the handle of the spoon.

If you use a translucent envelope, the card will look prettier.

BLACK TEA

You can make a small surprise message card using a tea bag for the card's envelope.

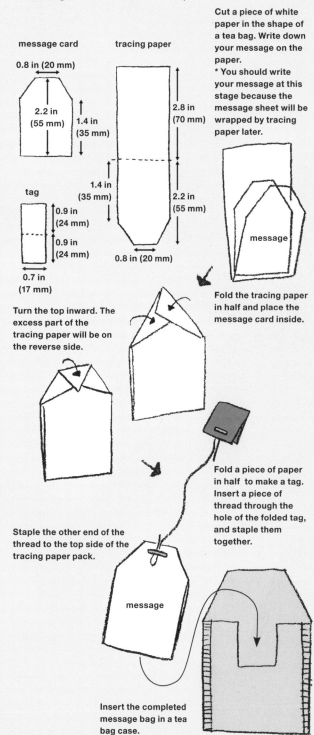

Cut a piece of white paper in the shape of a tea bag. Write down your message on the paper.
* You should write your message at this stage because the message sheet will be wrapped by tracing paper later.

message card

0.8 in (20 mm)

2.2 in (55 mm)

1.4 in (35 mm)

tracing paper

2.8 in (70 mm)

1.4 in (35 mm)

2.2 in (55 mm)

0.8 in (20 mm)

tag

0.9 in (24 mm)

0.9 in (24 mm)

0.7 in (17 mm)

message

Fold the tracing paper in half and place the message card inside.

Turn the top inward. The excess part of the tracing paper will be on the reverse side.

Fold a piece of paper in half to make a tag. Insert a piece of thread through the hole of the folded tag, and staple them together.

Staple the other end of the thread to the top side of the tracing paper pack.

message

Insert the completed message bag in a tea bag case.

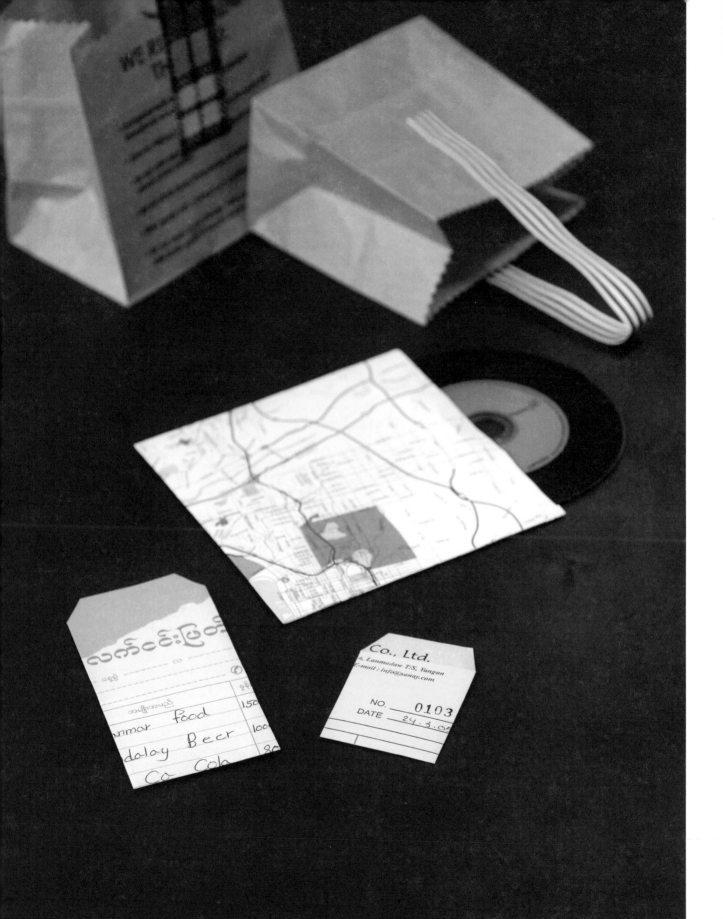

SMALL GIFT ENVELOPE AND CD SLEEVE

I keep gift wrapping paper, maps, and receipts from my foreign travels. They have attractive designs, and although they do not easily offer good ideas for reusing them, I devised one way to recycle them: by making small gift envelopes or CD sleeves with your favorite paper. Once you have made a template, you can easily create original items. If you make templates of various sizes, they can also be useful later.

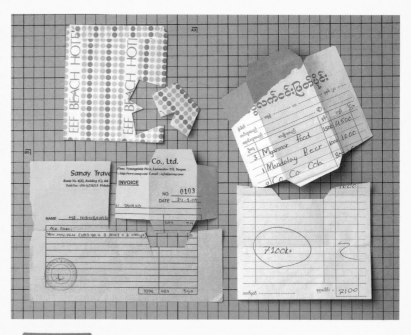

To make the Gift Tote Paper Bag shown on top of the left photo, see page 87.

Different ways of using paper

Apart from available paper and wrapping paper, recycled paper can surprisingly become a good material for creating charming house goods. Various kinds of paper items, such as hotel bills or supermarket receipts can be recycled. If you use several pieces of paper for a small gift envelope, the result can be prettier. Challenge yourself to create various paper goods!

MAKING A SMALL GIFT ENVELOPE AND CD SLEEVE

Materials
- Cardboard (for making the template)
- Colored paper, wrapping paper or maps

Tools
- Scissors
- Craft knife
- Cutting mat
- Glue
- Pricker
- Ruler
- Pencil

1 Make a template of the gift envelope using a piece of cardboard. Trace the shape of an unfolded envelope, or you can use the template shown on the opposite page.

3 Fold the paper and paste the flaps with glue to finish the small gift envelope.

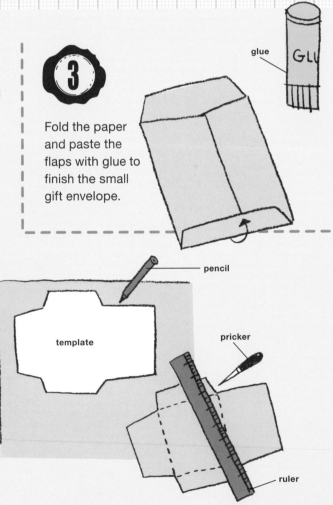

glue

pencil

template

pricker

ruler

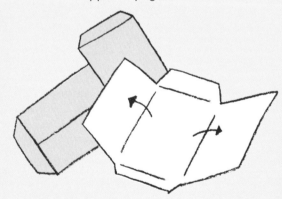

2 Place the template on the paper you have chosen. Trace the template with a pencil. Cut out the paper along the traced lines. Then, plot the folding lines with a pricker.

Cardboard template

If you do not have a small gift envelope, use the template below by enlarging it by 200%.

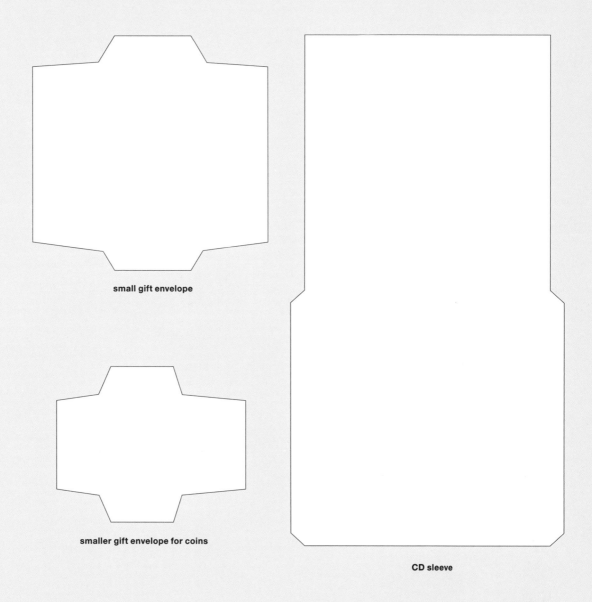

small gift envelope

smaller gift envelope for coins

CD sleeve

Enlarge by 200%.

MINIATURE ENVELOPE STRING BAG

I created miniature string bags from used envelopes. All you have to do is turn an envelope inside out and attach string handles on them. Some tax offices or public institutions use window envelopes with patterned designs on the reverse side. They also serve as artistic items. To make the handles, I recommend using linen string or linen cloth to add a nice texture. The miniature string bags shown here can be used as gift bags for candies, or as name card bags. They can also decorate your room as objet d'art.

To make the Dress Pattern Gift Wrap shown on the left, see page 86.

MAKING A MINIATURE ENVELOPE STRING BAG

Materials
- Envelope
- String

Tools
- Scissors
- Pinking shears
- Adhesive cellophane tape

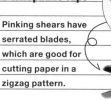

Pinking shears have serrated blades, which are good for cutting paper in a zigzag pattern.

pinking shears

STEP BY STEP

1 Cut the envelope flap with pinking shears.

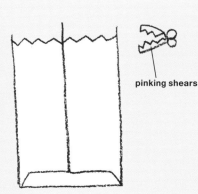

pinking shears

2 Turn the left and right edges of the envelopes inside, 0.6 in (15 mm), to make creases. Then, unfold the same edges. Fold the bottom edge of the envelope to make gussets.

0.6 in (15 mm)   0.6 in (15 mm)

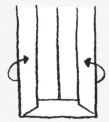
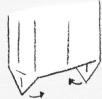
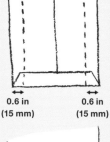

3 Tape the bottom side of the envelope with adhesive cellophane tape.

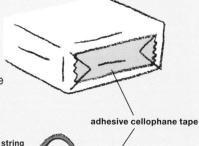

adhesive cellophane tape

string

4 Tape the string handles to the insides of the bag.

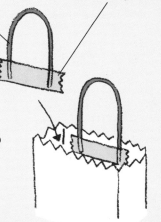

Some envelopes for electric bills have transparent windows and reverse sides printed in woven patterns. You can use these for the bag material.

Let's reuse bill envelopes! The reverse sides can be unexpectedly charming.

CONGRATULATORY GIFT ENVELOPES

These are casual-style congratulatory gift envelopes made from available envelopes.

MAKING CONGRATULATORY GIFT ENVELOPES

You can easily make these casual and personalized envelopes by just pasting paper napkins, paper lace, or buttons on them. I recommend using gold- or silver-colored materials for the envelope to make the presentation gorgeous. This gift envelope can be used not only to give money, but also to send out a letter. Alternatively, you can use the Small Gift Envelope introduced on page 80. Decorate the envelope with any accessories you like.

STEP BY STEP

H. Handmade Japanese paper envelope
I. Coaster
J. Corrugated ribbons
K. Strip of wrapping paper
L. Candy wrapping paper
M. Label tape

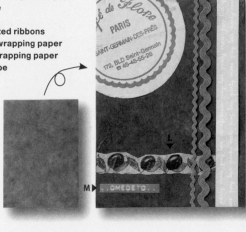

A. Stripe-patterned office envelope
B. Bird photo cut out from newspaper
C. Clipping from a bookstore paper bag
D. Paper doily
E. Paper napkin
F. Masking tape
G. Alphabet stamps

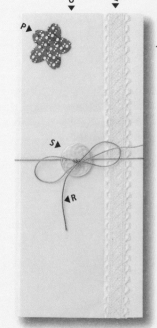

N. Japanese patterned paper envelope
O. Colored tracing paper
P. Japanese origami paper
Q. Lace ribbon
R. Elastic wrapping cord
S. French antique button

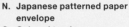

T. Plain white envelope
U. Flower photo cut out from a magazine
V. Iron-on embroidered seal
W. Silver lace ribbon
X. Confectionery package tag

DRESS PATTERN GIFT WRAP

This dress pattern gift wrap is easy to make and is suitable for packing candy gifts. It adds a special flavor to your presents.

Cut out a doll pattern from a piece of cardboard and decorate it with a seal and lace ribbon. Put the doll in a transparent plastic bag and tie a ribbon around the bag. Refer to the doll template shown at the end of this book.

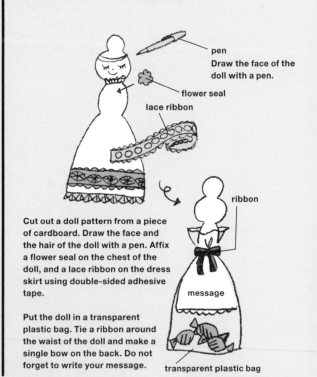

pen
Draw the face of the doll with a pen.

flower seal

lace ribbon

Cut out a doll pattern from a piece of cardboard. Draw the face and the hair of the doll with a pen. Affix a flower seal on the chest of the doll, and a lace ribbon on the dress skirt using double-sided adhesive tape.

ribbon

message

Put the doll in a transparent plastic bag. Tie a ribbon around the waist of the doll and make a single bow on the back. Do not forget to write your message.

transparent plastic bag

MESSAGE TAGS

This shipping tag can be used as a message card. You can loop it around the handle of a paper bag, or attach it to a gift.

Cut a piece of colored paper. Paste a piece of white paper on it to write your message. Refer to the template shown at the end of this book.

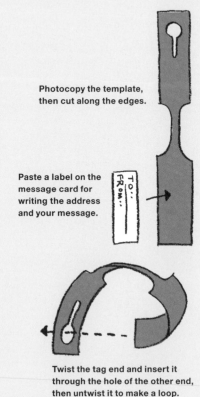

Photocopy the template, then cut along the edges.

Paste a label on the message card for writing the address and your message.

TO:
FROM:

Twist the tag end and insert it through the hole of the other end, then untwist it to make a loop.

GIFT TOTE PAPER BAG

An ordinary paper bag can look attractive if you attach a ribbon or a brightly colored paper strip as its handle. The gift tote bag shown here can contain small gifts.

Attach a handle on the paper bag using different kinds of paper.

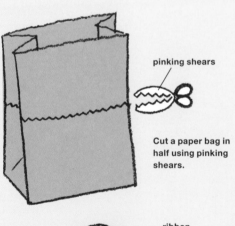

pinking shears

Cut a paper bag in half using pinking shears.

ribbon

Cut different kinds of paper or ribbons long enough to make the handle. Paste the paper or ribbon handle on the bag with a double stick tape.

WAX PAPER BAG

Some kitchen wax papers have nice textures, which are suitable for food gift wrapping.

Tear off a wax paper bag from the package. Cut along the dotted line, as shown below. Then, staple the handles.

The wax coated paper bag shown here is used for sandwiches, which is available at many stores.

craft knife

Cut along the dotted line, as shown below.

Cut both sides of the bag with a craft knife as indicated on the left drawing.

stapler

Staple two places on each handle.

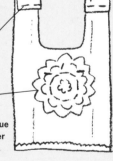

paper doily

Wax-coated paper cannot be pasted by glue or tape, so use a stapler to attach a paper doily.

WRAPPING PAPER AEROGRAM

Aerogram is a sheet of writing paper that is folded and sent out as a letter envelope. It is light-weight and economical. The recipient will be excited to open it from the perforated tear-off line.

Prepare a sheet of paper with a blank back. Cut out the aerogram in the size as indicated in the diagram below. After writing your message on the paper, seal the flap with glue. Perforate a tear-off line on the flap using a pattern wheel.

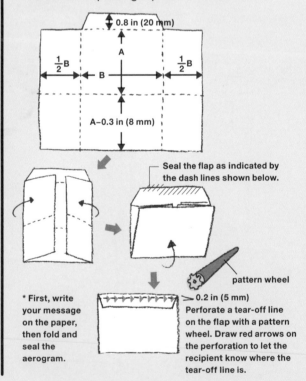

0.8 in (20 mm)

A

½B   ½B

B

A–0.3 in (8 mm)

Seal the flap as indicated by the dash lines shown below.

pattern wheel

* First, write your message on the paper, then fold and seal the aerogram.

0.2 in (5 mm)
Perforate a tear-off line on the flap with a pattern wheel. Draw red arrows on the perforation to let the recipient know where the tear-off line is.

FABRIC PICTURE POSTCARD

Paste a piece of fabric on a postcard. A patterned fabric adds charm to it. Draw an address box to make the card look attractive and personalized.

Paste a piece of fabric on a thick, postcard-sized paper, and draw an address box on it, as shown at the bottom.

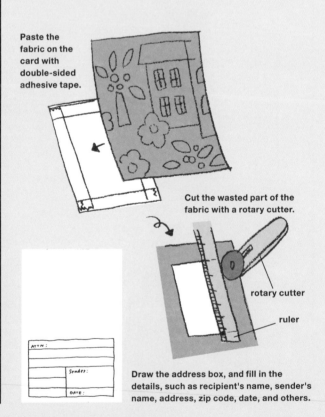

Paste the fabric on the card with double-sided adhesive tape.

Cut the wasted part of the fabric with a rotary cutter.

rotary cutter

ruler

Draw the address box, and fill in the details, such as recipient's name, sender's name, address, zip code, date, and others.

Having Fun at the Post Office

When I travel abroad, I never fail to visit the local post office. Every country has a unique post office atmosphere similar to a treasure house filled with parcel items in various designs. I find it exciting to look at those items, such as seals, envelopes, boxes, and other things. They are easy to make and are very functional. Some of them are even free.

I especially like the post offices in the U.S. and Singapore. In the U.S., I can get various items like document boxes, sturdy envelopes, and parcel labels. In Singapore, most post office items are not free, but they have a wide range of packing envelopes in good quality.

I like postage stamps, too, and buy many used ones.

I buy parcel items not just merely for my collection, but also for my actual consumption. I use them on business as envelopes for my illustrations. I use my collection of post office items for various occasions.

When I used to work in an office, I started to collect many cute items and use them in various ways. Since then, my charming collection has expanded immensely. Whenever I find a cute item, I cut it out and put it in my file. I found a name card case that is ideal for my filing system. Airline ticket stubs and other cute, little items fit perfectly in the pocket of the name card case.

I equate cute to "small." The illustrations on the body of large transportation vans may not look cute, but when they are reduced in size, they appear very charming. Convenient store logos can also be cute if they are reduced in size. I pick up these items from my file and paste them on stationery goods using adhesive tape, or use them to decorate greeting cards for my friends. The designs of the stationery items introduced in this book are all taken from my collection.

Look around carefully and you will find many interesting character designs for your stationery.

USEFUL DECORATIVE PAPER ITEMS FOR MAKING STATIONERY PRODUCTS

COLLECT CUTE DESIGNS, AND ILLUSTRATIONS THAT YOU FIND IN YOUR DAILY ACTIVITIES,
AND USE THEM TO CREATE MORE FUN HANDMADE STATIONERY DESIGNS.
BY PAYING ATTENTION TO THESE INTRICATE ITEMS,
YOU WILL BE ABLE TO DEVELOP YOUR OWN ARTISTIC SENSE.

TEA BAGS FROM FRANCE

I often receive this elephant-marked tea bag as a souvenir with a charming illustration at the back.

CHARACTER IMAGE ON ENVELOPES OF JAPANESE PUBLIC SERVICE INSTITUTIONS

The old character image printed on this envelope reminds me of Japan's Showa era (1926–1989). The character may be unknown but it is too special to ignore.

CAUTION SIGNS ON CARTONS

This carton may have come from China. I like the icon on the box because the design is unique and easy to understand.

POSTAL SEAL FROM FRANCE

I got this express mail seal at a post office in France that says "To be delivered within 48 hours." I think the design is good.

BUTTER CONTAINER CAP FROM IN-FLIGHT MEALS

I always take home the caps of various food containers served during in-flight meals, such as butter, jam, yogurt, and mineral water. Many of them have cute illustrations on the caps.

ILLUSTRATIONS ON JAPANESE BEAN CAKE PACKAGES

The illustration on this package tells the customers about the proper way of disposing Japanese bean cakes. The unsophisticated design makes the packaging attractive and eye-catching.

PEPPER SACHET FROM IN-FLIGHT MEALS

I find the illustration and characters on pepper sachets of in-flight meals very cute. The cozy-looking images and low quality paper are attractive.

CANDY WRAPPER FROM ITALY

This candy was a gift from Italy that was wrapped in a triangular shape and tied on the top. The wrapper material is similar to cellophane.

MY CUTE KNICKKNACK COLLECTION

PACKAGING MATERIALS

I keep all kinds of packaging materials, like confectionery wrapping paper, coasters, caps of cheese and milk packs, guitar string bags, salt, pepper and butter containers used in-flight meals, and others.

POSTAL AND PARCEL ITEMS

When I used to work in the office, my colleagues kept postage stamps and labels of parcels from foreign countries for me. Since then, I have been collecting postal and parcel materials. These are mostly used postal items cut out from cartons or postmarked items.

TRAVEL ITEMS

When I travel abroad, I keep air, bus, and train tickets. I also collect tags, trash bags, and public printed matters. Once, I even picked up a used bag on the floor of an airport. I welcome anything that attracts me even if it is a lost article.

CHARACTER ITEMS

I like both Japanese and foreign character illustrations. There are some Japanese characters that come from transport companies and drugstores. Many characters project good images. Some may be unknown but attractive, and can be found in instruction notes inserted in souvenir packages. I cut out these illustrations and stock them in my file.

MY CUTE KNICKKNACK COLLECTION

AFTERWORD

During the process of developing ideas for new stationery items and testing their use several times while writing this book, I realized that handmade stationery can be made without spending too much money on it, but it requires a lot of creativity. Consequently, it makes you happy even if the item you have created is small.

My actual specialization is drawing illustrations and developing ideas for miscellaneous goods that are to be printed or mass produced. Therefore, creating stationery items piece by piece, and by hand, involved a totally different process for me.

However, I had so much fun in cultivating my imagination and using my own hands to make the items presented in this book. Now, I cannot stop creating more objects.

AUTHOR'S PROFILE

Kazumi Udagawa

Born in Tokyo, in 1970, Kazumi Udagawa graduated from Musashino Art University, Tokyo. As a designer, she worked for a sundry goods maker, and focused on product planning and development to start up a goods store. Currently, she is a freelance designer for various home products, supplies, and design projects. She also creates illustrations for books and magazines.

APPENDIX AND PATTERN TEMPLATES

How to Use the Pattern Templates

This section contains the pattern templates and drawings for the stationery ideas I have presented in this book. You can make photocopies of them, or cut them out directly. Certainly, you can develop your original designs based on these templates and drawings.

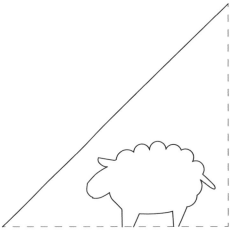

Easy-to-make Stationery Items

ASSORTED BOOKMARKS
ENVELOPE CORNER BOOKMARKS

page 63

Make a photocopy of the pattern and align it to the corner of the envelope. Then cut with a craft knife.

Cut along the solid line.

To cut out the animal shape, insert the cutting mat's corner inside the envelope and cut only one side of the envelope.

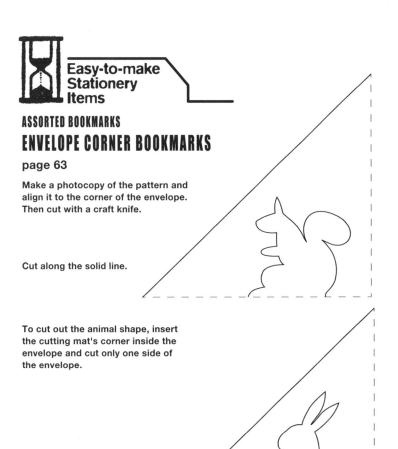

Easy-to-make Stationery Items

THINGS-TO-DO MARKERS

page 66

Cut along the solid black line.

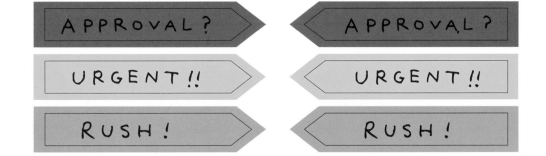

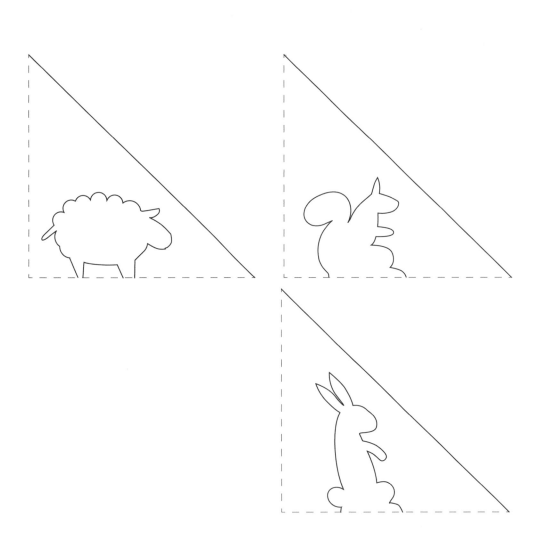

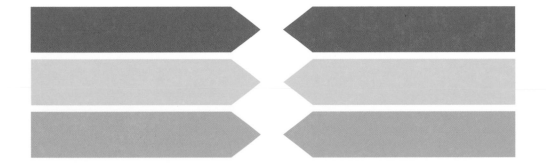

GREETING CARDS

page 77

Cut along the solid black lines.

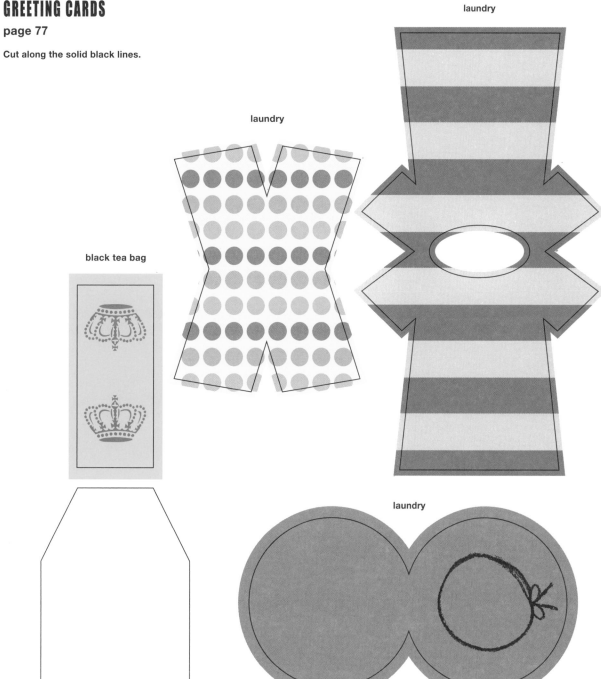

laundry

laundry

black tea bag

laundry

Easy-to-make Stationery Items
GREETING CARDS
page 76-77

Cut along the solid black lines.

butterfly

coffee

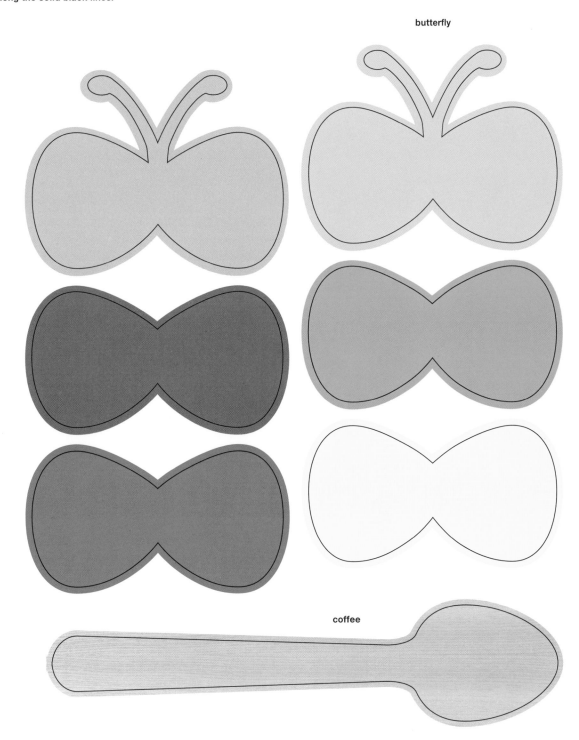

Animal Postman: Bear
Cut along the solid black lines.
Make slits along the dotted lines.

Animal Postman: Bear's letter
Cut along the solid black lines. Write
your message on the back of the
card. Fold the card into four parts,
and insert the message between the
bear's arm.

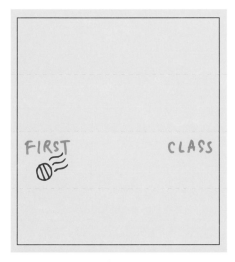

FIRST   CLASS

Dove
Cut along the solid black lines.
Make slits along the dotted lines.

migratory ride on the updrafts created when southwest-facing cliffs of the Rocky Mountain's Front Ranges reflect the sun's heat. Think of those eastern-most ranges as wind farms, and you'll be thinking like a raptor, or at least one that's booked a direct flight from as far north as Alaska to a winter retreat in the southwest States, or even Mexico. —

Twice a year, the ancient ritual unfolds over Jasper National Park. Twice a year, I've been captivated by the graceful majesty these eagles display as they shadow the wind sometimes kettling-up – wings stretched wider than I am tall with wingtips fingering gentle breezes – before leaving one range for another, other times gathering ferocious speed as they kite along ridgelines, wings slightly tucked. It's a thrilling site to behold.

Easy-to-make Stationery Items
GREETING CARDS
page 76

Dove's letter
Cut along the solid black lines. Write your message on the back of the card. Roll up the message card and insert it between the slits.

Easy-to-make Stationery Items
PAPER CLIP HOLDER HEDGEHOG
page 65

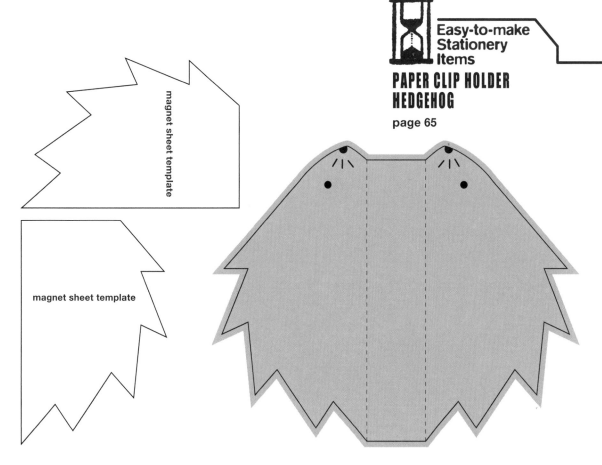

magnet sheet template

magnet sheet template

Photocopy the magnet sheet template below. Place the copy on the magnet sheet, and cut out the magnet sheet along the lines.

Cut along the solid black lines. Fold on the dotted lines so the paper will stand.

Easy-to-make Stationery Items

MESSAGE TAGS

page 86

Cut along the solid black lines.

Write your message and your name on the labels and paste them on the tag.

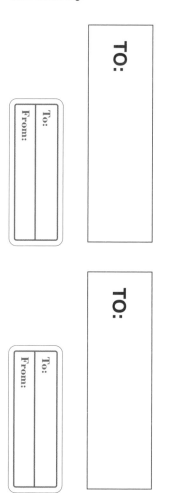

TO:

To:
From:

TO:

To:
From:

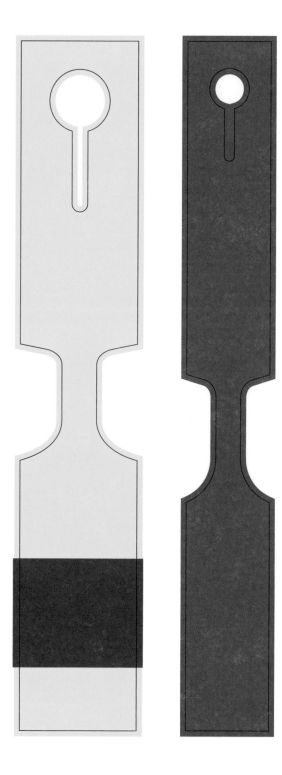

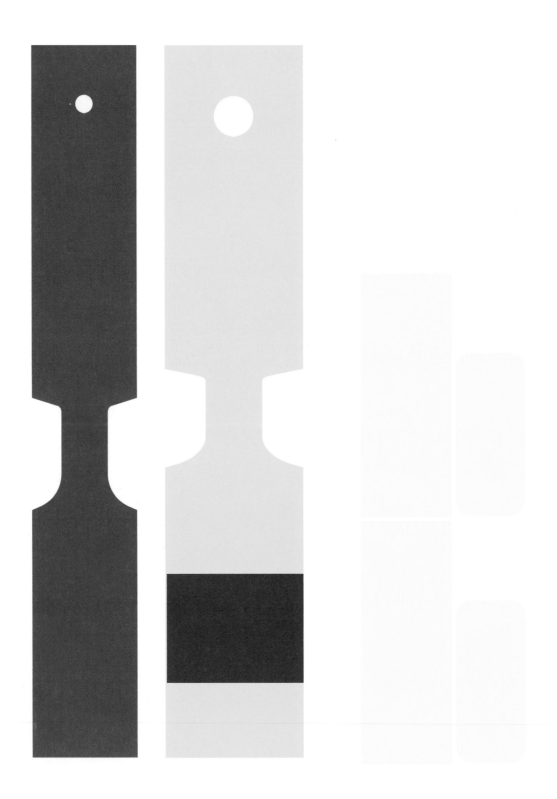

DRESS PATTERN GIFT WRAP

page 86

Cut along the solid black outlines.
Do not cut the doll's face.

HORSE-SHAPED CARD CLIP

page 67

Cut along the solid black outlines.